Driving Engagement

trust, communication, and action to accelerate your team from 0 to 60

Eric Liechty and Marcus Williams

Williams & Co. Publishing

Table of Contents

Preface

One of our primary motivations for writing this book was our desire to help new leaders understand how they can maximize the productivity and effectiveness of their employees by increasing engagement and supporting mental health.

As a leader, we want you to think back to your first leadership position and how you felt as you transitioned from employee to leader. What did you want to accomplish? What did you hope to change or improve? Ultimately, did you feel like communication with your leaders was effective? And if not, would improved communication have helped your transition into leadership?

We are very excited for this book and believe the principles contained herein will resonate with you as we compare business leadership to something you probably use every day—cars. After reading this book, every time you sit down in a car or walk through a parking lot, you will think of the leadership principles you learned in these pages.

We enjoyed many animated discussions and brainstorming sessions as we built the chapters of this book. As we discussed how to best broach the topic, we went down many rabbit holes comparing everything from tie rod ends, brakes, and wiring harnesses to business positions and structure. Ultimately, for the sake of simplicity and the highest impact, we will use two different metaphors throughout the book.

1. Employee as driver - Each employee drives their own career. Those who

work for or with them help keep their car (career) running.

2. Leader as driver - Closely related to the first metaphor, each leader drives their own division, conscientiously listening to every part of the car (their various employees) to keep their division running at peak performance.

In each scenario, the business owner supplies the vehicle, which is important to note, because the choice of vehicle is of paramount importance—more on that later.

As a leader, you are driving your own car, or career, but also driving the division you oversee. Life suddenly got complicated as you assumed leadership responsibilities. But never fear. The lessons you have learned from driving your employee car will help you become king or queen of the road on your fabulous road trip to leadership success.

Chapter 1

Getting Behind the Wheel

"*T*here I was, traffic whizzing by, broken down on the side of the road. My whole day was shot."

Does that sentence conjure up any memories for you? Maybe memories you would rather forget? How about this one:

"*It was a typical crazy Monday morning. I was running late (as usual) and was mentally rescheduling my day when I sat in the car and turned the key to...nothing. The car simply refused to start.*"

For all of us who just expect that when we turn the key, our car will start and take us where we need to go, car trouble can be a great cause for anxiety. We know we have to feed the car gas and get the oil changed whenever the dashboard computer tells us it's time, but otherwise, it is supposed to just *work*. Just the thought of having to take our car to the shop for a few days—to say nothing of astronomical repair bills—can be the source of massive anxiety and financial stress. You may, like many people, trade in your car every few years just to avoid this anxiety. You would rather have a perpetual car payment than have the *thing-a-ma-whatsit* go out on you at the worst possible time.

Where else will you find the same type of anxiety? What else in your life do you wish just worked? Your job? Your team? And why does it always seem to break down at the worst possible moment—like when you have a looming deadline or when you're about to launch a new product? As a leader, you are responsible for yourself, your employees, and your team's production. With so many moving parts, it's no wonder so many leaders get stuck.

The world is changing. We are experiencing a massive paradigm shift in the workforce, arguably one as big as the Industrial Revolution; it's time to think differently.

Employees are no longer willing to put up with a crappy job just so they can collect their pension in forty years. Employees no longer feel loyalty to their employer or gratitude to them for providing a job. Employees no longer grin and bear it.

Your people, the workforce of America, are demanding something better.

LOST RESOURCES

So far in this massive shift, things aren't getting better. According to Gallup[1], in 2022, only 34% of workers were engaged in their jobs. A full 16% were actively disengaged. Think about that. Only around two thirds of your workforce is even minimally engaged at work. Think of the lost resources represented in those two numbers. You, as a business leader, are essentially driving a car that is firing on only one cylinder.

---

1. https://www.gallup.com/workplace/388481/employee-engagement-drop s-first-year-decade.aspx

You are paying salaries, benefits, 401K contributions, facilities costs, and more to people who don't even want to be there.

The US Bureau of Labor Statistics lists current employee tenure at an average of only 4.6 years.[2] On top of that, it costs an employer about one third of the employee's salary when they leave.[3]

Between lack of engagement and high turnover, employees are costing American businesses billions of dollars every year. This begs the question: why do we continue to pay two-thirds of our employees to sit at work, unengaged and unmotivated? We are giving money away, like filling up the gas tank and then letting the car idle in the driveway all night.

Do you believe your unengaged workers are happy, that they somehow believe that they are pulling the wool over your eyes—sticking it to the man? Of course not! Levels of anxiety and depression are through the roof in our society. People want to enjoy their work. After all, we spend the majority of our life at work. We went to school for a career we thought we would love. We followed our passion, and our passion turned into the cause of our depression. What went wrong?

Employees are facing increased demand and expectation, more than ever before. There is no off switch. We no longer live in a world where you punch a clock after your eight hour shift and not think about work again until morning, especially not in the gig and service economies.

Our employers expect us to be available at any time, day or night. We are constantly connected:

"No work today, I promise," I told my wife as I carried our daughter's birthday cake out to the patio. I lit the candles and everyone gathered to sing "Happy Birthday."

---

2. https://www.bls.gov/news.release/tenure.nr0.htm

3. https://www.apollotechnical.com/employee-retention-statistics/

Just as she leaned over to blow out her five candles, my phone buzzed. My wife looked over at me and gave me that look. You know the one. It buzzed again. I shrugged and took the phone out of my pocket. Just as I feared, it was my boss.

"I know it's your daughter's birthday, but we just got a call from our client. I'm gonna need you to get that proposal done today. Sorry."

I sighed and returned the phone to my pocket. This kept happening. For every time my employee promised "family comes first," I can name a time they have disrupted a birthday or vacation. But what could I do?

My wife followed me back into the kitchen.

"Don't you dare," she hissed. "Not again. You promised her."

"I'm sorry, honey. What can I do? Quit? We have a mortgage."

"If you go to work today, you can take a suitcase and sleep at the office," she declared.

"But..."

"No," she finished, turning abruptly to return to the party.

Ring any bells? And we wonder why our employees are unhappy and unengaged!

"Employees with a good work-life balance are 10% more likely to stay at their companies."[4]

When productivity is down, or turnover is high, it is time to pay attention. The Check Engine light is glaring us right in the face. It is time to pull over and diagnose the problem before it's too late.

MISSING RESOURCES

---

4. https://www.tinypulse.com/hubfs/2018%Employee%20Retention%20Report.pdf

One word: communication. How much are we missing due to poor or dysfunctional communication? Are you, as a leader, constantly and honestly communicating with your team members? Do they feel safe to come to you with problems or concerns?

You hired each employee for their specific skills and experience. Are you truly utilizing those skills? Have you invested in their progression?

Think of a time you were assigned to a project or position different from the job you accepted. Maybe it was in a completely different field or discipline, and you were expected to magically become proficient in that skill without any formal training or guidance.

Or perhaps you were assigned a project with no guidelines, deadlines, or parameters. Then, when you completed the project, you were castigated for not doing it correctly. Would it have been so hard for your boss to communicate his expectations along the way?

Let's take that thought a bit further. Have you ever felt you were being underutilized or improperly utilized? If only you and your coworker could switch assignments, you would both be happier; but you don't feel comfortable going to management and expressing those thoughts and feelings.

"There is a 16% decrease in retention rates for employees who aren't comfortable giving upward feedback."[5]

MULTIPLE MASTERS

As a leader, you still remember what it was like on the employee side. You can still draw on those negative experiences and feelings you had as an employee. Maybe that's why you decided to move up into leadership. You wanted to make a

---

5. https://www.tinypulse.com/hubfs/2018%20Employee%20Retention%20Report.pdf

difference, to be the change you have always wanted, to be the leader you wished you had.

Then reality hit. You actually don't have that much power. In fact, instead of serving one master, you now serve two.

You are feeling pressure from your employees to do the things you always talked about. But you never realized how much pressure you would be receiving from corporate, from your new boss.

Marcus

> I recall a new-leader training I once attended. They brought in a senior corporate leader to give us a rousing welcome speech. Do you know what I remember from his message? He said (and I paraphrase), "You're on our team now. It's us against them."

Wait. What? I thought we were all on the same team.

That's the old way of thinking. Us vs. them; management vs. workers. Those are leaders who don't understand the new workforce paradigm. They come from a time when they, the bosses, ruled supreme. It was their company, and you were being paid to do a job, so do it, and don't forget to shut up.

That doesn't work anymore. They aren't the only game in town. Employees will call their bluff and walk out, looking for greener pastures. Then what? How is that leader going to continue building and creating without a workforce?

The pressure you feel is real. It gnaws at you. You find yourself popping antacids like candy. You feel torn. You try to juggle your roles: protect your employees while keeping your boss happy. But no one can juggle forever. Eventually, your car runs out of gas and you are stuck in the middle of nowhere on the side of the road.

THE SHIFT

Just as we expect our car to safely take us to our destination every time we turn the key, we want our team to accomplish their goals with unquestioned consistency. We want every part of the car to do its job, from the brakes, to the sensors, down to the wiper fluid. With the proper knowledge, diagnosis, and upkeep, it is 100% possible.

You don't have to trade in your car every two years because you fear having to deal with repairs. With the proper upkeep and maintenance, you can create accurate expectations, make repairs when needed, and drive that car safely for 200,000 miles, or more.

With the proper balance of trust, communication, and action, you can create a workforce that is engaged and productive.

Up until now, the CEO was always in the driver's seat. He would turn the key in the morning and expect us all to fire up and get to work. If a part broke down, he would replace it and move on. Employees were expendable, replaceable parts. But no more.

Today, leaders must grow to understand that it is truly the employees who drive the company. Each part is vital for the company to operate at peak efficiency. With proper care and maintenance, the CEO, with your help, can make the company growl like a well-tuned muscle car or cruise over obstacles like a souped-up SUV.

Chapter 2

Shifting Gears

"*W*ait a minute," you say. "*This isn't some sort of workers' collective ownership type of book is it?*"

Absolutely not!

This is a new way of thinking, a complete paradigm shift on the role of leadership, framed in a way to which we can all relate.

We are all familiar with cars. We may not understand exactly how they work or what every part, sensor, or wire does, but we know that when we turn the key the car starts, and when we put it in drive and push on the gas, it goes.

When you finish this book, every time you get in your car to go to work, go shopping, go to a game, or go on vacation, you will remember how you, as a leader, play an integral part in keeping your company running.

Here's the thing: A CEO can have the greatest idea or product in the world, but without employees who show up every day to do the work of making the widget or writing the code, that idea can never be realized.

This concept that employees are necessary stems from the labor movement, where workers organized for better wages and better working conditions. But we are past that. The business world has evolved. Up until the Industrial Revolution, businesses were local. Goods and services consisted of what was locally available based on talent and resources. Your occupation was chosen as a result of your location and family. Your dad was a blacksmith? Well, guess what? You're going to be a blacksmith too.

During the Industrial Revolution, new factories created a massive number of jobs in centralized areas. People relocated to the cities to work. Now, instead of your job being the result of your location, your location was a result of your job. Generations of people lived and died in cramped urban centers because they were tied to their employment.

But now the world has gone digital and virtual, a shift which was accelerated by the restrictions imposed because of COVID-19. Suddenly, you don't have to live in Washington to do your job for Boeing. You can sit in your home office in Wyoming, staring out at the Grand Tetons, while you attend a virtual meeting. Everyone realized, in a moment of collective epiphany, that the centralized office was a leftover remnant from the factory age.

Of course, many jobs require workers to be present. You can't manufacture widgets remotely. Despite advances in technology, humans are still required to pack and ship boxes or check on machines, and in some cases, even attend meetings. Plumbers can't unclog a toilet through the Internet. Roofers have to actually be on the roof to lay shingles.

Even so, attitudes have changed. Workers have realized that they are not tied to one company in one location for their entire working career. As companies moved to save money by reducing pensions in favor of 401K plans, they also cut the ties that bound their employees to them. In one fell swoop, they significantly reduced payroll cost while at the same time caused a massive employee-retention crisis.

We all know the grumpy uncle or neighbor who suffered through work five days a week for 40 years so he could collect a pension. He constantly complained about his job, his managers, and his company. He was miserable for 40 years of his life just so he might be happy for the final 10 or 20.

It's like the person who drives the old, run-down car but always complains he can't afford a new one. Instead of putting money into a new car, every month, he puts more and more on his credit card as he pays for repairs and parts to keep the old jalopy running. By the time the car finally dies, he has put enough money and time into it to have purchased a brand new car many times over.

That attitude is gone!

As a leader, you no longer have automatic employee loyalty (even if that loyalty was involuntary). Everyone knows if they don't like their job or their location, they can just move and find a new one. Refer back to the time-in-job rate cited earlier—only 4.6 years. The median tenure for younger workers, age 25–34, is only 2.8 years! [1]

So, here's where you as a leader have to shift your thinking. The founder or CEO is the one who decided on just the right car. What, dare you ask, is the "right" car? Well, the right car has to fit the field and the organization to attract the right kind of employees. Is the company more of a pickup truck, or is it a shiny new Lamborghini?

Take a minute and grab a pen and piece of paper. Now, list the companies you have worked for. In the next column, assign those companies a car. See? You

---

1. https://www.thebalancecareers.com/how-long-should-an-employee-stay-at-a-job-2059796

were probably able to exactly match the culture, mission, and product of each company with a certain type of car. Some employees want a reliable, simple sedan. Some want something rugged and adventurous. Others prefer flash and speed.

The CEO chooses what type of company she wants the company to be and then is in charge of building it. Unfortunately, leaders too often think employees want a sports car, so they build a shiny sleek body, but then try to force fit it onto the frame of a truck or SUV, something that more accurately reflects the mission or product of the organization.

It doesn't work. The only way the vehicle runs smoothly is if all of the parts match and work together. If you purchase a sports car and find it drives like a truck, you take it back. It did not meet your expectations.

If the car is designed and built well, the right employees will be drawn to it, just like crowds at a car show. People know what they want. People know where their skills will fit in and be best utilized.

But the CEO's job doesn't stop there. She now has to create and maintain the driving experience. She has to provide the daily energy required to keep all of the components operating smoothly. More on that later. She is responsible for ensuring maintenance is done on time and bad parts are replaced with good ones when necessary. She has to build the right process, system, culture, and environment.

She has to create an environment where the employees are given the freedom to roll down the windows, turn up the radio, and drive.

She can build the most expensive and beautiful company in the world, but if no one shows up to make it run, it sits in the garage gathering dust until the tires go flat and mice move into the seat cushions. As a leader, you have a critical role in creating and maintaining the driving experience within your roles and responsibilities.

When you turn the key to your car, it doesn't "just start." You set off a complex sequence of events that finally result in the engine roaring to life. You are now an integral part of that sequence of events.

When you realize that employees aren't just replaceable cogs in an assembly line, but that they bring specific and individual skills, talents, and attitudes with them, you will begin to understand that your role as a leader is to construct an environment in which they can thrive. When you create a place where people want to be, where they feel valued, where they feel they are being utilized effectively, they will hit turbo and want to optimize their performance.

Let's talk now about what has to happen to keep that car running at maximized performance.

Chapter 3

Trusting the Components

E^{ric}

I recently had a customer bring in their car with a report that their vehicle died while driving. My first step was to check the battery, which, as expected, was dead. So I tested and charged the battery. Everything worked fine. Two hours later, the car was dead, which led me to diagnose that the alternator had gone out. Your car's battery is rechargeable, just like those batteries you use in your remote or your kid's toys. Everytime the car runs, the alternator recharges the battery so that your car will start after sitting overnight. I replaced the alternator, and my customers took the car home, everyone confident it was fixed. But then they called me saying the car died again in the driveway. So I dug a little deeper and asked some additional questions. Come to find out, there were cranking and ignition issues. It wasn't just the battery after all. I had been fixing only part of the problem.

So, who was at fault in this situation? Both of us! I assumed they had given me all of the information, so I didn't ask any follow-up questions. I made a diagnosis based on what I was told and ended up treating only part of the problem. On the other hand, they didn't do a good job of describing what was going on either. They came to me to fix their problem, but were unable to articulate what that even was, wasting time and money. We had a communication problem.

We all hear a lot about the importance of communication. There are whole systems built to encourage 360° feedback. So, why do they fail more often than not?

Effective communication requires two key components:

Trust and Expectations

Again, when you sit down in the driver's seat every morning, place your drink in the cupholder, and adjust the radio from whatever noise your teenager was listening to, you fully trust that the car will start when you turn the key or push the button. You expect your car to get you from home to work. Your car expects you to supply the fuel and input to make that happen.

Think about it. What if your car was alive and able to speak to you? What if it talked throughout the entire journey instead of just sending signals to lights on your display? What would it say?

"Hey buddy, ease up on the brake pedal a bit. That hurts."

"You know, I'm feeling a bit stiff. You think you could stop off for a quick quart of oil?"

"Seriously, my glasses are so dirty I can't even see. How about some washer fluid?"

"Wooah there, I'm feeling a bit naked. You left some of my tire rubber on the street going around that corner."

Now, ponder this question: If you were able to provide perfectly honest feedback to your employer without any fear of repercussion or retaliation, what would you say? Do you feel free to say that now? The answer is *no*, because, well, the answer to that question very rarely happens to be *yes*.

Now, no one is advocating a free-for-all. You may remember the movie *Liar, Liar* starring Jim Carrey, where he was unable to tell a lie. It destroyed his personal and professional relationships. In this context, we are talking about the freedom to provide honest, tactful, professional feedback. You were hired to do a specific job, and you should have the freedom and permission to provide feedback and information pertaining to that job.

Every sensor in a car has a purpose. One sensor cannot be substituted for another. Someone with a different job should not be telling you how to do your job and vice versa.

Expectations

In order to give your employees the freedom to do their job and communicate freely, they must have a clear understanding of what that job entails and what you expect. Setting expectations starts at the very beginning of their relationship with the company, before they are even hired. You start setting expectations in the hiring process.

If you show up late to the interview, you are communicating and setting the expectation that tardiness is acceptable. If you take a week to respond to an email or phone call, you are setting the expectation that it is okay to ignore messages. You are communicating your expectations in everything you do and say, especially in those first few weeks.

As a leader, you are responsible for setting expectations about work, culture, and effective communication.

Have you ever gone into a job having no idea what is expected of you or what you are supposed to do? Imagine if a car manufacturer just soldered together a bunch of random wires and chips and plugged them into the car. What would you say when the car wouldn't drive? Would you purchase that car?

When you hire, you are trying to fill a specific need in the business. You need someone with a specific skill set to do a specific job, whether that job is just placing widgets on a conveyor belt or filing legal briefs in federal court. If the widgets don't get placed properly, your product doesn't reach completion. You know what you want this person to do, so tell them.

Why is it always a secret? Why do we constantly put employees in situations where they don't really know what success looks like? It's like the IRS. They know exactly how much you owe in taxes, but instead of just telling you, they make you go through an arduous, unintelligible process of trying to figure it out on your own, so that when you make a mistake, they can fine you. Who thinks that is fun—or even rational?

When you set clear expectations for job performance, your employees feel comfortable knowing exactly what is expected of them. Now your job is to honor the skills you hired them to use. You've replaced the belt on your engine, now let it run!

Clear expectations not only create employee freedom, they allow for professional accountability.

As a leader, you are empowered to fix problems or tweak your team because everyone has a clear picture of their role. There is no misunderstanding. You can respond to an employee's failure to meet expectations in a predictable and reasonable way. If a part breaks, you can fix it or replace it as necessary.

Depending on the role, expectations may consist of specific goals and metrics, or they may be more broad. For example, maybe the employee has to assemble so many widgets per hour, or make so many sales calls per day. These are the vehicle parts with specific jobs. The fuel-level sending unit has two jobs: measure the amount of fuel in the tank and send that information to the fuel gauge. It would be ridiculous to ask it to also measure the oil level or turn on the headlights.

On the other hand, tires are expected to deal with widely varying and quickly changing situations. They hold the car up when stationary. They have to be ready at a moment's notice to drive over asphalt, concrete, gravel, detritus, rain, snow, or ice.

Although you would measure the effective performance of both parts differently, they both know exactly what their role is to make the car run. And, most importantly, both components are essential; neither is more important than the other.

Trust

How many times has our fuel gauge done its job communicating to us that our fuel was getting low, and we ignored it? It even turns on a little yellow light in hopes of getting our attention, but we still ignore it.

Marcus

> I once purchased a used truck, which I thought had a low fuel light. It didn't. So one morning I jumped in and started driving to work. I saw the fuel was low, but assumed a light would go on if it got "too low," so I ignored it. When the truck sputtered and died halfway to work, I was able to safely pull off of the road. I called my wife. This is roughly how the conversation went:

> *"Hello?"*

"Hey, sorry for waking you."

"Okay, what's going on?"

"Well, I have good news and bad news. Which do you want first?"

"Uhmm, how about the good?"

"Well, I know exactly how many miles the truck can go on one tank of gas."

"That's good to know. What's the bad news?"

"It won't go a single inch further."

Pause

"Oh, so you're saying you ran out of gas and need me to bring you some?"

"Yep."

My fuel gauge was doing its job. I had an expectation that was not part of its job description (the light) and chose to ignore its feedback. If that gauge had been an employee, do you think they would come to me the next time they had a problem to report? Why would they bother if I was just going to ignore them anyway?

Your employees must see that you are listening to what they say and then doing something about it. If they come to you and tell you they need a certain tool or resource to fulfill the expectations that you provided, it is your job to fill that need. It is your job to stop and get gas or inflate your tires.

No matter the size of your company, there are dozens, if not thousands, of moving parts. Those parts have to operate every single day for you to run and be profitable. And guess what? Parts are going to break down or lose efficiency.

Don't panic. Don't slam on the brakes in the middle of the freeway because your tire pressure light came on. Trust your team to communicate the problem and propose a solution.

Trust yourself by trusting the people you hired.

Marcus

I once had a job where they communicated to me that my feedback was welcome. They told me that they recognized me as the expert in the field and wanted to learn from me. I was the only person in the entire organization with my specific skill set, knowledge, and experience. I took them at their word. At first, things were great. But soon, I had to start providing feedback that was contrary to their beliefs or expectations. At one point, I was forced to cite my expertise to tell them they had just taken the wrong exit and were driving straight over a cliff. It was then, when my expertise was most needed, their true colors came out. Apparently, they were only interested in positive feedback, affirmation, and validation. As soon as they made a wrong turn, my feedback was no longer wanted.

Feedback

When you provide timely and honest feedback regarding your employees' performance, they start trusting that if they haven't heard from you, they must be doing a good job. They know you will tell them if they need work or improvement. Don't wait until the annual performance review to give them a list of things they need to work on. Set an example of open and ongoing communication by providing fair, honest, and timely feedback in a constructive way.

You will find that as you have these small conversations, your employees will start opening up as well, providing you the feedback you need to fulfill your expectations.

Just as Eric learned with the battery and alternator, don't be afraid to ask questions and dig a little deeper. Find the root of the problem so that you can fix it. Otherwise, you will find yourself spending all of your time on superficial fixes that do nothing to improve your team's performance, culture, or morale.

Don't keep driving when the check engine light comes on. Head to the nearest shop and get the diagnostic code. Again, don't panic. It may be as simple a fix as tightening the gas cap. But it also could be something that will cost you hundreds of dollars if you don't take care of it right away.

Your employees will only communicate freely and honestly if they know what is expected of them and trust that you will listen and act when they communicate with you. Your car might not be able to speak the way you do, but when there's a problem, you need to listen to what it has to say.

Chapter 4

Heeding the Sensors

Not only is your vehicle designed to function as advertised, it has an entire system created to communicate to you when something needs your attention. Your vehicle has multiple built-in reminders and warning systems to help you prevent catastrophic failures.

However, your vehicle cannot fix itself, at least not yet. We are living in a world where self-driving cars are a reality and may soon become mainstream. Nevertheless, even the most technologically advanced car won't drive itself to a maintenance center at night only to be back in your garage ready to drive the next morning. Perhaps one day.

Safety systems are only effective if you, as the owner of the car, listen to them and take action. Even when parked, your vehicle may have built-in safety or security features. Do you have an alarm system installed? Is your car equipped with an anti-theft start system? Something as simple and mechanical as the parking brake can keep you safe.

Marcus

I had a truck with a manual transmission. It was parked in my driveway, the gear shift in 1st gear to keep it from rolling down the slight incline. But I failed to engage the parking brake as well, and my daughter, who was probably eight or nine years old, decided to play in the cab. She hit the shifter and knocked it out of gear, causing the truck to roll backwards. She was able to jump clear, and thankfully no one was behind the truck at the time except for the neighbor's poor mailbox. But my failure to utilize a simple safety feature could have ended in tragedy.

According to the United States Department of Transportation, frontal airbags saved 50,457 lives between 1987 and 2017.[1] Now cars are equipped with side airbags as well. You don't need to buy a luxury vehicle to get features such as airbags, automatic braking, blind-spot monitoring, anti-lock brakes, and more.

Apart from these automatic safety features, our cars have built in warning systems. You may see the dreaded Check Engine light on your dash, among others. The sensors in your car are tasked with identifying problems and then communicating those problems to the operator. It is up to you, as the driver, to get the problem diagnosed and fixed.

How many times do we think we're the expert and refuse to listen to what the car is trying to tell us?

Eric

I recall a time when a customer called and said his vintage truck was vibrating horribly. He was convinced the problem was the motor mounts, a major repair job. As the trained mechanic, I started asking additional questions, trying to rule out other, more simple solutions. I thought it could be his tires. One of the ways a vehicle communicates that the tires are going bad is they start to vibrate. Instead of a light on the dash, you hear and feel the warning. But the owner of the truck refused to listen. He

---

1. https://www.nhtsa.gov/equipment/air-bags

was on the phone arguing with me, convinced it was the motor mounts, when BOOM, I heard a loud noise over the phone. The man said he had to go and hung up. Later I learned he had blown a tire.

Getting new tires was a simple solution, yet he refused to believe what the truck was telling him and what his mechanic was telling him. Had the tire not blown, he would have spent a lot of time and money changing the motor mounts when all he needed was new tires.

When it comes to our vehicles, we receive feedback through all of our senses. We can check tires or fluid levels with our eyes. We hear squealing belts or grinding brakes with our ears. We smell burning rubber with our nose.

Eric

I recently had a woman bring her car into my shop with the engine overheated and damaged beyond repair. She said the Check Engine Light had come on weeks ago, but she thought she could wait a couple of weeks to get it checked out. In the meantime, fluid leaked onto her garage floor and other warning lights came on. Unfortunately, she ignored them all until it was too late.

```
 CHECK
 ENGINE
```

As a leader in your company, you must learn to recognize warning signs that indicate a system, team, or process is breaking down. You must trust your warning systems to give you the information you need to act, whether that be routine maintenance or a big repair job.

Fatigue—Stress—Low Production—Low Morale

These are all warning signs that something is wrong with your company, and whatever is causing it needs to be fixed.

One of the most common leadership responses to these warning signs is to blame the employees, which is simply a way to rationalize not taking action or responsibility.

- Employee suffering from job fatigue?

They need to stop going out at night and get more sleep.

- Employee stressed at work?

Maybe they should have planned better and not taken that family vacation when there was a deadline looming.

- Your team suffering from low production?

It's just this new generation; they're all lazy.

- Signs of low morale?

Well, at least they have a job; why are they complaining?

By ignoring the warning signs and reassigning blame, you are only exacerbating the problem—and what good does that do? Your employees become less and less productive, and your business suffers.

What if you shift your thinking?

- Employee suffering from job fatigue?

Maybe they are not in the role they are most qualified or suited for, thus leading to apathy and low job satisfaction?

- Employee stressed at work?

Maybe you have not provided them with the resources they need to do their job to the standard they would like?

- Your team suffering from low production?

Maybe your systems are outdated, confusing, or redundant.

- Signs of low morale?

Maybe your team keeps telling you they need help, but they don't see you taking any action.

There is no business on the planet that is perfectly run or designed and will never have problems. Even brand new cars require maintenance and repairs.

As a leader, you must create an environment that encourages employees to report problems, provide feedback, and send you the important warning signs. Don't send an email encouraging everyone to report problems and then expect it to just happen. You have to show your employees that you value their input by taking action whenever a problem is reported to you.

What would happen if someone got so sick of their Check Engine light coming on, that they just disabled it? Does that make the reason for the light go away? Of course not!

Marcus

> When my daughter called one day to tell me her light came
> on, I told her to drive straight to the auto parts store to have
> a technician read the code so that we would know exactly what
> was wrong. Knowledge would allow us to make smart decisions.

When you rectify problems early and quickly, you demonstrate your willingness to keep your company in fine-tuned, working order. You value every employee and the part they play in making the business run.

Sometimes the action you take is to repair or replace a faulty part. In the workplace, this could be an employee who is violating your policy, acting inappropriately, or simply not in the right place. A part made for one car won't properly work in another. If you are facing this situation, you must handle each case consistently and equally.

Sometimes your employees are going to do bad things, things that hurt other employees or your business. They can become a poison that infects the entire team. Take sexual misconduct for example. When one person engages in sexual harassment or assault in the workplace, it impacts not only the victim, but the entire workforce. It's like disconnecting the brakes from your car and telling everyone not to worry, that the car will still drive fine.

When misconduct is reported:

1. You must initiate a professional investigation immediately.

2. You must ensure the safety of all parties during the investigation.

3. You must act upon the findings of the investigation.

Even if the accused is your friend or best worker, if the investigation finds that the allegations are supported, you have a bad part in your car that must be replaced. One of the most fatal mistakes in business leadership is thinking that employees who are deemed "important" get a pass and are allowed to continue working, while so-called "unimportant" employees, accused of even lesser offenses, are fired.

Guess what? When you do this, you are communicating loud and clear that you are only going to heed the warning signs that interest you or impact you personally. Faulty rear seatbelt? No big deal. I never sit there anyway. Well, what about the person who does?

As a leader, constantly watch, listen, and feel. Use every tool at your disposal to diagnose and rectify problems as soon as you learn of them.

Learn to anticipate and avoid problems, just as you perform scheduled preventative maintenance on your car. Are your employees all in the role that is the best fit for them?

Marcus

I once worked for an organization where the same job title encompassed a very large job description. We were expected to be proficient at everything, but encouraged to become experts in a specific function. At one point, I was assigned to fill a role that had sat vacant for some time, and was going to lose funding if not filled. Although the role was technically included in the job description, it was world's away from the expertise I had spent over a decade acquiring.

I worked in the role for a short time, and knew immediately that I would not be able to provide the level of production or service the role deserved. Sure, I could do the minimum, but it would take years for me to get to where they wanted the person in that role to be. As a result, I was not happy, but instead of throwing up my hands and declaring that my employer was getting the product they deserved, I made a case to my supervisor why my talents and skill-set were being wasted. As a company asset, I could be utilized elsewhere with much better results for me and the company. It took time, but eventually they realized that they had spent time and money building an expertise that was currently being wasted.

Most employees won't come to you. They will simply resign themselves to do a job they have no desire to do, and do so with less and less enthusiasm as time passes. You should be actively engaged in communicating with your employees and making sure they know that your goal is to put them in a role where they will be engaged and productive.

Chapter 5

Finding the Key

W hat is the key to your success? What is the key to your business? To answer those questions, you first need to discover the key that activates your employees.

Ponder the following to find the answer to important questions:

Why do people want to work for you?

Is it your

- vision,

- product,

- pay,

- leadership,

- field or industry,

- or culture?

Why would someone want to work for you? Is it because you are a nice person, or is there something more?

The answer is probably a combination of the above, but everyone will have a ranked order of priorities. Ultimately, everyone wants to enjoy the car they are driving (the work they are doing). According to a Philips Work/Life survey, "68 percent of working Americans would be willing to take a salary cut to work in a job that better allowed them to apply their personal interests to the workplace."[1]

As we see from this survey, and many others, the key ingredient to creating successful and engaged employees is to find their key: the personal connection that keeps them happy and engaged at work.

Someone may think they want the keys to a sports car, but after driving it around for a while, they realize they would be much happier with a pickup truck. We often hear people say, "Find your passion and turn it into your career." This is a great sentiment, but our passion isn't always a skill or product that will pay the bills. Sure, it would be great if everyone could make a living from doing their passion, but everyone has multiple interests and desires, and those change over time.

You are a business leader, not a career counselor. However, in a way, you are able to guide or help your employees find the role that meets their needs by fulfilling their "why." Maybe they love a certain technology, and you can provide that experience. Maybe they love your vision. Maybe you inspire them, and they just want to work and learn from you as a mentor.

If you want to learn more about the power of leadership and culture in attracting the people most fit for their organization, take some time to study the different leadership styles of Richard Branson and Elon Musk.

When pondering how to find the right keys for your employees, ask yourself another question:

Do you satisfy their need to thrive?

---

1. https://www.usa.philips.com/a-w/about/news/archive/standard/news/pr ess/2013/20130517-Philips-Work-Life-Survey.html

This doesn't just mean that you provided them with the proper tools they need to do their job. Are you creating the right environment and giving them the freedom to hit the gas and go? Don't downplay the importance of providing the right tools. You can't hire a software engineer and fail to provide an adequate computer or connection, just as you can't hire a mechanic and expect him to work without wrenches.

You need to be thinking outside of the box. If one employee will be more productive working from home than in the office, what is wrong with allowing it? Not everyone has the same key. Some love an open, collaborative environment, while others thrive in a private space. Learn how your people work most effectively, and then figure out ways to make it happen in a way that meets your needs as an employer.

Stop coming up with reasons why you can't do something and start thinking of ways that you can. Show your employees that you want them to enjoy their work as much as possible and are willing to provide what they need.

Many companies have jumped on the culture bandwagon and decided that if they make the workplace "fun," people will be more likely to stay, work hard, and enjoy their jobs. They provide free meals, gyms, daycare, game rooms, and more. Before you spend the money on turning your office into an arcade, really consider whether that is the key for your team at large. Who, if anyone, is going to feel more fulfilled at work if they can play ping-pong whenever they want? How many employees will benefit from an on-site daycare? Would it be better to just provide vouchers to those who actually need it? How many office gyms are used more by dust mites than employees?

Those benefits are nice, sure, but are they *the key*?

Many companies lure in prospects by offering flashy benefits that quickly sour when the employee tries to use them, doing more harm than good to the company. One such benefit is unlimited paid time off (PTO). Sure, it sounds great, but employees quickly learn this is more a benefit to the company than the employee. Employees have to request time off, which is rarely granted, or if it is, comes with heavy layers of guilt for leaving your teammates in the lurch. The company saves money because there is no accrual of PTO and in turn, no payout when an employee leaves the company.

According to Rob Whalen, "Unlimited PTO sounds generous on a job description, but employees by and large end up getting paid less with no value attributed to their PTO while companies gain more of their employees' prod uctivity."[2]

Maybe unlimited PTO is the key for your employees. Regardless, you need to ask yourself some hard questions before changing a policy or investing in a new, shiny benefit. Are you doing it for your employees or your bottom line?

Do you <u>want</u> your employees to be happy, content, and fulfilled—for real?

You will never discover the key to your employees if you don't actually care. Is this just a talking point for you, or is it one of your core values? How many companies tout their family friendly environment and then expect every employee to be on call every second of the day? Have you ever had a boss who called you during an important event and said something like this:

---

2. https://workforce.com/news/unlimited-paid-time-off-is-a-deceptive-pl oy-in-todays-workplace

"Hey, sorry to bug you on your time off. I know you're getting married today, but I had a question about that spreadsheet you turned in yesterday."

Does that boss really care about you or your family? Of course not!

You can't be all talk. You have to truly make an effort to learn the key to each employee's fulfillment and productivity; and then, you need to do whatever you can to provide that key. If you truly value that employee and the work they bring to your team, you'll find a way.

Generally, this isn't something that is going to cost you a ton of money. Remember, your employee applied for the job. They asked to work for you. At least in the beginning, they wanted to be there. You just have to create a reason for them to stay.

Are they willing to get the car repaired when it breaks down, or will they immediately start looking for another ride?

The answer to that question is largely up to you. If you have created the car they love to drive—if they are in the right job and in the right environment—they will be willing to work with you to fix a problem so they can stay.

When someone junks a car at the first sign of a problem, you know they never found their key, whether that be your fault, theirs, or a combination.

Ultimately, the best way to identify the key is to listen with humility and true intent. As we discussed earlier, put your employees in the driver's seat. You are building the vehicle they need to succeed and giving them the opportunity to drive their role to success.

What is their key? Remember: finding their key is ultimately the foundation of your success as a leader.

Chapter 6

Addressing the Failures

Y ou've heard the phrase: "Timing is everything," but have you really thought about it?

Your car's movement is wholly dependent on multiple things happening in succession and in the correct order. Many cars have an RPM gauge on the dashboard, but do you really know what that means?

In a small car, the RPM, or Revolutions Per Minute, means that a 4 cylinder engine has 4 controlled explosions per one revolution. So, a car that travels down the road at 3000 RPM is having 12,000 controlled explosions per every one minute of driving. If you have a bigger vehicle with an 8 cylinder engine, that number doubles to 24,000 controlled explosions in one minute of driving. That is not 12,000 revolutions or turns; it's 12,000 explosions.

BOOM!

Depending on the size or scope of an employee's role, they may be dealing with dozens of decisions and tasks every day. As a leader, do you truly understand all that your employees do in their time at work to move the organization forward? As a vehicle moves us from one location to another, we fuel and maintain the vehicle, trusting that all those controlled explosions will continue to happen every minute to get us to where we need to go. In fact, most of us never even think about all those little forces that get us from A to B.

No two car parts do the same job. The pistons can't do the job of the valves and vice versa. The explosions only happen when every part is functioning properly, independently, and yet in sync with the whole.

When one of those parts breaks down or wears out, you have to have it repaired or replaced. You might be on a long journey with a demanding deadline, yet as soon as you hear the vehicle misfiring or not acting as it should, you have to find the nearest service station and pull over. We all know that breakdowns always happen at the most inopportune times and in the most inconvenient places. That's just a fact of life.

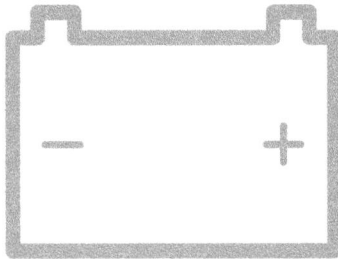

Marcus

I recall when I was a newlywed. We owned an old beater Dodge Omni and were driving from Utah to Southern California. We stopped for gas in Baker, CA. If you've ever driven on the I-15 freeway, you've seen the giant thermometer at Baker recording the insanely hot temperatures in Death Valley. When we finished filling up, the car wouldn't start.

We found someone who agreed to jumpstart the battery, and the car fired right up. There were only a few hours left in our journey, and we didn't have the money or desire to spend additional time in Baker, so off we went. A few miles down the road, there was a rest stop. The car started losing power as I was driving, so I was able to pull into the rest area, where it died completely.

I don't remember if we had a cell phone at that point, but even if we had, there would not have been any service that deep in the desert. Luckily, there was a pay phone at the rest area, and we called my father-in-law, a mechanic who lived in Southern California. He immediately diagnosed our problem as a bad alternator, and agreed to grab a new battery and drive out to meet us.

There we sat, in the heat of the desert, while he drove the 2 ½ hours to meet us. He changed the battery, and we were able to make it all the way to his home on the new battery's charge. What should we have done? Well, first of all we should have checked the condition of the vehicle before leaving on our journey and conducted preventative maintenance. But let's say we did that and still didn't catch the bad alternator. The wise choice would have been to recognize the signs when we were at the gas station in Baker, instead of fooling ourselves into believing the car had died for no reason.

But we were poor college students, newly married, and living on a shoestring budget. At the moment, we could not see how we would be able to afford a hotel room in Baker or a mechanic. Luckily, my father-in-law was close enough to help. Without him, we would have paid even more for a long tow to Barstow in addition to repair costs.

We just wanted to make it to the end of our journey, so we were too stubborn to stop along the way to take care of the issue. We just needed the car to hold together long enough to make it to our destination.

Does this sound familiar? Does your business live and die by deadlines: contracts, shipping, deliverables, advertised release dates? The list goes on. As a leader, you just need your team to hold it all together until you reach the next all-important deadline.

But sometimes, the best way to meet a deadline tomorrow is to pause and fix an issue today. When you feel someone on your team sputtering, or you notice the timing is off, don't ignore it. Don't convince yourself it will be fine. Otherwise, you will find yourself stranded in Death Valley.

Are you willing to blow up your entire engine just to reach one goal? Where does that leave you in the future? How do you expect to make it to the next step if you blew up your team to reach this one?

Change your thinking. You aren't losing time and money when you stop to make a repair; you are saving time and money in the future while maintaining the operability of your car. When you step back to fix an issue, you may actually increase the efficiency of your team going forward. You may replace that 4 cylinder engine with an 8 cylinder and move ahead faster than you ever imagined.

It's always great if you can repair a broken part. If your employee is struggling to fulfill his or her role efficiently and timely, you have to diagnose the problem and decide how to move forward. Maybe you have them in the wrong place, as if you plugged the wrong fuse into the wrong socket. On the other hand, you may find that your employee belongs to a truck, and you're trying to drive a sedan. In some cases, you may find that the part is unrepairable and needs to be replaced.

Sometimes the best service you can offer an employee can be the most difficult for you to give. In these instances, the best answer is to let them go. The truth can hurt, but if they are in the wrong place, you are ultimately doing them a service.

How you do it matters. A poor repair job doesn't do the trick. Act in humility and firmness when you share the news. Of course, you must follow the guidance of your HR department, but remember that you are talking to another human being, and it could very well be you in that position one day.

Don't speak in meaningless corporate shoptalk. Provide honest feedback with true sincerity. As their leader, you see things they don't. You may see where they would be a better fit, even if they haven't quite figured it out yet for themself. If they agree to accept it, offer your honest opinion. Share where you see them being the happiest and most productive. It may be the first time someone has ever given them honest feedback.

Our entire lives, we are told we can be whatever we want to be. Rarely does someone say we will be happiest doing what we are good at in a role where we feel the most satisfaction. The two may not be the same thing.

Marcus

> I wanted to be a pilot growing up, but after studying the requirements and lifestyle required of pilots, I knew I wouldn't be happy. The job did not fit the lifestyle I wanted to live.

As a leader, you are responsible for identifying and fixing a problem before it becomes a catastrophe. Avoid the tunnel vision of deadlines and benchmarks. If you fail to maintain your car, it will operate for a time, but it will eventually explode—and you may not be able to avoid getting stranded on the side of a long road.

Chapter 7

Keeping it Running

We've talked about your employees sitting in the driver's seat and the importance of putting them in the car that best matches their disposition and position. But don't forget, you are also an employee. Even if you are the founder and owner of the company, you still work for the brand. That means you are also a driver.

What kind of driver are you?

Do you baby your car? Do you own a monthly membership at a car wash? Maybe a car wash isn't even enough for your car, and you detail it yourself every Saturday morning. Are you hard on your car, demanding it to operate at maximum performance every day? Do you accelerate fast and brake hard, weaving in and out of traffic? Maybe you own an off-road vehicle and are always trying to climb a steeper hill or larger boulder.

Do you push the needles on your dashboard into the red, maxing out the RPM and controlled explosions?

Now, consider how you drive your team. Are you pushing your employees to max out their abilities, energy, and motivation? Or do you treat them with kid gloves, constantly worried you might offend someone if you demand too much?

When your team is facing a project deadline or a sales goal, there are many ways to motivate them to reach those goals. You can work them until they drop, or you can motivate them to perform their role with pride and diligence, so that every part of your machine, or your car, is working together.

Are you willing to "kill" your engine to achieve success?

Many leaders operate that way. They view employees as expendable parts. If one breaks down or quits, they go to HR and demand another be hired, just like going down to the local parts store to buy a new fuse or gas cap.

There is a massive cost to that way of thinking, not only the cost of recruiting, hiring, and training, but the cost to reputation and culture. When you treat employees as expendable, they start seeing themselves as expendable.

Where is the motivation to do their best work when it could still get them fired? What is the point in putting in maximum effort for a boss who does not appreciate you or see you as a valued member of the team? When you drive your team into the ground, it is not just your business that suffers. Their relationships, mental health, and physical well-being also suffer.

By operating with that mindset, you are essentially destroying the vehicle just to meet a short-term goal. Unless your company is doing something so amazing that you have a line of qualified candidates banging down your door, you can't afford to create a culture of expendables.

The entire point of finding the right vehicle for your employees is to maximize the execution of their own unique skill set, one that you have already decided you need in order to operate. After all, you originally hired them because of the potential you observed in their initial interviews.

You did not hire a software engineer to manage your production floor, just as you didn't hire a salesperson to hide away in an office all day to write code. It is amazing how often employees are assigned to do jobs that they not only don't have any desire to do, but ones for which they have no competency.

When you look at your organization chart, if you see an empty position next to one that is double stuffed, that doesn't mean you take one of those "extra" employees and just plug them into the empty slot. You can't use an airflow sensor as a fuel sensor.

As an employee, you certainly are responsible for driving your own career. You have to find the right fit and driving style for you. But you can't focus solely on yourself if you want a successful, fulfilling career.

When you also think of yourself as an integral part of your leader's car, responsible for the efficient operation of your system within that car, you begin to understand the importance each person plays in your team and the importance of diagnosing and maintaining the vehicle. It is in the best interest of your career for your entire team to be successful.

When you take care of your vehicle, it will last much longer.

Marcus

> We recently decided to purchase a newer vehicle. When we went to the dealer, they asked if we had a vehicle to trade. We replied that we did, but doubted they would be interested in the trade. When the dealer asked why, we explained that the car we were driving was originally owned by a mechanic who took exceptional care of the vehicle, and it had well over 500,000 miles on it.

After overcoming the initial shock reaction, the dealer agreed that he could not accept the vehicle as a trade, but that he would love to put it on display in his dealership, just to show customers how reliable his cars were! We all had a good laugh. That vehicle didn't drive that many miles because it was a certain make or model. It drove that far because the driver followed a strict maintenance and diagnostic schedule and never allowed a small problem to become a big one. Sure, the vehicle wasn't worth anything on trade, but it more than paid the difference over the years when others were buying new cars and we didn't have to.

Be self-aware.

Take inventory of your leadership style and how you are driving your team. Is it sustainable? Will your team make it 500,000 miles before it has to be replaced? Or will you have to pay to replace it every other year?

Chapter 8
Signaling Quickly

It's not just the boss's fault.

You may currently be in a leadership role, or you may be preparing for one. Either way, you are also an employee. Very few people in this world answer to no one; even those at the top answer to shareholders.

This chapter is for employees, so put on your employee hat. When you implement these strategies, you will become a better employee and a better leader.

Every employee has a job to do or role to play in the company, just as every sensor or part on a car is integral to it running efficiently, or running at all for that matter. While some car parts are luxuries, others are added to comply with laws or regulations. The car might run without those parts, sure, but it would not be legal.

It doesn't matter if you were hired to work the grill at a restaurant or to write complicated code for your company's groundbreaking AI software, you were hired to do the job so that your leader doesn't have to.

When HR created the job announcement, they did so because the company determined it was worth the money and resources to hire someone to fulfill a specific assignment. Out of all of the people who applied and interviewed for the position, you were chosen as the best candidate. Your skill set was needed to perform a specific task or role.

We have already talked about why it is important to keep employees in the role for which they are best suited. That is not at issue here. By virtue of the fact that you were hired to perform a specific job based on your specific skills and abilities, you took upon yourself the burden of ensuring your job is done correctly.

That's right. It is not your manager's responsibility to ensure your job is being done properly. You were hired for that purpose.

The automatic headlight sensor on a car is designed to detect and turn on the headlights when needed. It cannot do the job of the tire pressure sensor. The tire pressure sensor can send a signal to the computer that the tire pressure is low. The computer then activates a light in the dash notifying the driver. Then, the driver has the responsibility to pull over to the nearest service station and add air to the tires.

So yes, the driver may be responsible for fixing the issue by adding the air, but the driver will never know the tire pressure is low if the sensor does not accurately and efficiently communicate that information back through the car's diagnostic system.

If you were given sixty seconds to write down all of the problems in your company, or more specifically, all of the resources you need in order to do your job better, you could likely draft a fairly comprehensive list. No job is perfect. There are always ways to fix problems or do tasks better.

Now ask yourself, "Have I ever communicated that list of concerns to my manager?"

Employees love to complain, but they rarely take the steps necessary to fix any of their complaints. Your manager cannot fix a problem she is not aware of. In the next chapter, we will focus on how a leader can foster an environment of open communication between the sensors (you) and the computer (your leader).

As issues grow or continue unresolved, morale dips and problems become the favorite topic of conversation between employees. That does nothing but foster discontent. Complaining to your coworker might make you feel better, but it does not allow your leaders the opportunity to fix the problem. It would be like the tire pressure sensor sending the low pressure signal to the automatic headlight sensor and then complaining the driver never stopped to fill the tire with air. The driver will keep driving until the tire goes completely flat, or worse, blows, and then the tire pressure sensor blames the driver for the catastrophic failure. But if the signal was never sent...

Providing feedback can be scary and uncomfortable, but as an employee, you have a responsibility to communicate the help you need to do the job you were hired to do.

Marcus

> I once worked for a government agency that had all sorts of problems with employee behavior, leadership behavior, and morale. The behavior included unethical and even criminal acts. I did the job I was hired to do, yet consistently received feedback that I shouldn't be working so hard or creating so much work. My boss never came out and said to not do my job, but she still made it very clear she would prefer I lessen her workload by not doing more work than was absolutely necessary.

This was my first "grown-up job," and my mind was blown. I had no idea how to react. I couldn't believe the culture of laziness and downright corruption. Luckily, I was able to find a group of other employees who had pride in their work and cared about doing a good job. I latched on to them but quickly began looking for another job.

I should have known better, because one of the first things said to me when I reported for my first day of work was that I wouldn't last long in the job. That seemed an odd thing to say to a new recruit. But as time wore on, I understood the comment. No one with any motivation or pride in their work stayed there for long.

I attempted to provide feedback and to fight for the tools I needed to do my job better, but it mostly fell on deaf ears. Eventually, I found another job and gave my notice. As part of the exit package, they gave me a feedback form to fill out regarding my experience working there. It was clear the form was just a formality. No one actually cared what I had to say. But I took the assignment seriously. I wrote a long document answering all of the questions on the form and detailing all of the roadblocks I faced in doing my job.

On my last day, I brought in my completed survey. Because I knew it would just be thrown away, I made copies and placed it in the mailbox for every single leader in the agency, hoping maybe one would actually read it. I could not honestly walk away from the job without providing my insight on why their turnover rate was so high. They hired me to do a job and then blocked me at every turn until I had to leave. I felt I had a responsibility to share that information, and so I put the ball back in their court, so to speak.

So, what happened? Well, I don't know if any changes were ever made based on my feedback. But I did find out years later that the woman who originally asked me to fill out the survey was so angry that I had shared my feedback with the entire command staff that she tried to get me fired from my follow-on position. One of my friends had to stop her and remind her she was opening herself and the entire agency to liability if she did so. I am definitely grateful my friend had my back.

So, what's the lesson there? Sometimes your leaders may not give you the tools you need, and sometimes your position becomes untenable, and you have to leave. Hopefully, if your leader has read this book, that won't be the case. But that does not excuse you as an employee of the responsibility to diagnose problems within your realm of responsibility and then report those problems up the chain.

Don't wait for your boss to ask for feedback. Don't wait until the tire blows and then say, "Oh yeah, the tire's been flat for the last 150 miles. Sorry." You will see the problems first, and the earlier you report them, the earlier the problem can be diagnosed and fixed.

Leaders have a great responsibility to give their employees all of the tools they need to do their jobs. But as employees, let's stop blaming leaders for our every problem. Instead, let's be part of the solution. How?

Approach with the problem *and* a solution.

When you notice a problem within your job or team, you have the responsibility to report it right away. We've already established that. But remember, you are the expert in that role. It's possible, if not probable, that your boss has never done your job and couldn't do it even if he wanted to. Telling him there's a problem is a good first step, but that does nothing to resolve the issue.

Let's be honest, your boss may want to fix your problem. But if he has no idea how, it is very unlikely he will have the humility to come back to you and ask. Leaders don't want to look weak or stupid in front of their employees. Ironically, humility shows strength, not weakness. But again, we will talk about effective leadership in the next chapter.

Just assume that your boss needs your help. You are the subject-matter expert, so you should be involved in developing the solution to whatever problem you've reported.

Whenever you report a problem, always present one or more potential solutions to the problem. Explain what you believe could resolve the problem and why. But don't make demands. Approach with humility. Show your boss that you just want to do the best job possible for the company and this is one way you feel you could provide better results.

They might implement your solution, or they might go another route. Either way, by providing that option, you will have demonstrated that the problem was real and that there were viable ways to fix it. You got the ball rolling. In the end, what matters is that your leaders were able to make your job better because you presented a problem and provided a solution in a way that helped them understand it was in the company's best interest to get it fixed.

Can you drive on a low tire? Sure. But you are risking a blowout and decreasing the life of your tire. It is in the driver's best interest to spend five minutes now at a gas station adding air rather than replacing tires down the road. It is the sensor's quick communication that allows the driver to remain safe and prevent a much bigger problem.

Chapter 9

Learning to Drive

As promised, it is now time to discuss diagnostics and feedback from the leader's perspective. Now that you understand that your employees have a duty and responsibility to provide you with feedback and potential solutions, it is your job to build the environment or culture where that can happen.

Many leaders are afraid of feedback or suggestions from their employees. They don't want to look weak or stupid, so they communicate with everyone around them that honest feedback isn't welcome. We saw that in the example in the previous chapter. The employer provided an exit survey, but didn't want the employee to actually fill it out and turn it in. That was very clearly communicated through experiences in the job and also the way in which the survey was provided—more as a requirement than as something that was valued.

Your employees are brimming with thoughts and suggestions on how to make their workplace better—more efficient, more productive, and more fulfilling. They talk amongst themselves. They start sentences with phrases like: *if only. . .wouldn't it be great if. . .* and *if I were CEO for a day...*

You should be asking, "Then what? What would you do if you were CEO for a day?"

But most employees never share those well-thought-out, meaningful ideas with you because they don't believe you want their feedback, or they are afraid of how you will react if they do provide feedback.

Marcus

I once had a manager who was a bully. He yelled and screamed at his employees. He berated them in front of others. He had expectations that were not only outside of the job's scope, but were unreasonable and made no sense. He talked down to everyone, both inside and outside the organization. He did not accept any feedback. None of his employees would even dare approach him.

I had the unfortunate privilege of having the office right next to his, and I heard every screaming rant and watched employees leave his office in tears. I also heard his phone calls to his boss, where he frequently lied about what was going on in his division.

One day, we had what they called an "office inspection," which entailed his boss coming in to review our work and interview each employee on how things were going. It was billed as this great way for two way communication and feedback. Sounds great, right?

Not so fast. As she sat down in my office, the first words out of her mouth were that she did not want to hear any complaints about our manager unless he had committed a felony. Then she proceeded to ask me how everything was going.

Well, the answer was that she was in charge of a sinking ship. Things were terrible. But how could I share that with her when she explicitly told me not to complain about my manager? So what did I do? I shut down. I lied and said everything was fine, just to get her out of my office. I could have puked when the inspection report came out a few weeks later reporting everything was fine and dandy.

Imagine if you bought a new car and the first thing you did was cut all of the wires leading to the dash. Maybe you find all of those little lights annoying when you are driving at night, so it was just easier to get rid of them. Then you jump in your car every day and, without a care in the world, drive around in ignorance, never realizing that you have sensors trying to communicate with you.

The check engine light was on. The check oil light was on. The low tire pressure light was on. But you saw none of the warnings because you chose to disconnect the lights for convenience' sake. The dash looked better without all of those annoying lights.

That is essentially what happened during the office inspection. She purposely muted every sensor (employee) so that she could write a glowing report. The office fell under her supervision, so a negative inspection would have reflected badly on her. She couldn't have that.

A car is built to trust that when it throws a check engine light, a conscientious driver will take care of it. Why then, in a work setting, do we not listen to our employees? We ignore the check engine light because we don't want the negative image, the extra work, or the uncomfortable situation. Many leaders would rather allow an entire team to implode than to fix an internal problem.

You have to create an environment where your employees feel comfortable providing feedback.

How can you do this?

    1. Listen.

    2. Request.

    3. Ask.

    4. Act.

LISTEN - When an employee comes to you with a problem, take the time to listen and truly understand what they are telling you. Don't try to act like you know everything. Remember, they were hired to do that specific job because of their specific expertise. Allow them the time and courtesy of your undivided attention. If you aren't following, have them continue explaining until you do understand. You should be able to explain the issue effectively to your boss.

REQUEST - Tell your team that you want their input and expertise. Ask them to always come to you with a potential solution to every problem. Don't promise them that you will implement their specific solution, but allow them the ability to think through a solution. Even if you don't use it, it will be an invaluable tool to help you and your bosses come up with a good solution. If they come to you with a problem without a solution, ask them what they would do if they were in your position.

ASK - Ask questions. How does this impact your work? How does it impact others? Is this just a problem in your role, or is it an issue for the entire team? How did you discover this problem? Do you have data to back it up that I can take to my boss? What is the financial impact? How is this affecting morale? The only way to truly get to the root of the problem is to show that you care by asking questions and allowing your employee to share all of their thoughts.

ACT - Once you have knowledge of an issue, you have a duty to act. The most effective way to shut down honest feedback is to do nothing with it.

Marcus

> I have been involved in many employee surveys. I recall one in particular when an issue impacting almost the entire workforce was hurting morale. They sent out a survey, and we all eagerly filled it out with our input and suggestions. As employees, we talked amongst ourselves and knew we were all submitting similar feedback. However, months later, the leadership sent out a message claiming the results of the survey showed that everyone was happy and no changes would be made. We were in shock. There was no way that was an accurate reflection of the survey results.

> So, what do you think happened the next time a survey came out? No one filled it out. We knew that they would not take any action on our feedback, so what was the point in providing it?

The anonymous suggestion box has to go. Having an anonymous suggestion box is an open acknowledgement that you have created an environment where employees do not feel comfortable providing feedback or suggestions to their boss. It is an open admission of failure.

There will be a difficult transition as you try to get your employees to trust you with their thoughts and feelings. The best way to build that trust and confidence is by following the four steps outlined above. Show them that you need their expertise and that you recognize they have knowledge you don't.

Get rid of the attitude that your position somehow makes you more special or intelligent than your employees. Show your employees respect, both personally and professionally. Show humility by acknowledging you need them for your team or business to succeed. A great driver isn't the one who can do the engine's job the best, it's the one that knows how to listen to the machine and keep it running. Once the employees see that, they will feel invested in the business in a way they never were before, which will naturally increase productivity, morale, and ultimately profitability.

Chapter 10

Choosing a Driving Mode

I sn't it interesting that the most "my way or the highway" type leaders are also the most incompetent? There's a saying you might hear if you were working as a government employee: "promoted to his highest level of incompetence."

For some reason, people who want to be promoted tend to focus more on promotion than they do on learning the ins and outs of the company and its product or service. They want the bigger check, the distinguished title, and the power. All across the country, organizations are promoting the people who want to be promoted rather than the people who deserve to be promoted.

Why is that?

Being a great leader requires humility.

The more humble a person, the less likely she will believe she is worthy or ready to lead. So, that puts us in a quandary. We need those people to lead, and we need them to recognize they are ready and capable of doing great things.

Take a moment to honestly examine why you wanted to become a leader in your organization. Did you do so out of a desire for the check, title, and power, or did you have more altruistic motives? Do you truly believe you can help your employees be more engaged and more productive? Do you have ideas that will increase retention and create a culture where people are knocking down your door to work for you?

Where do you fit in the leadership triangle below?

Humility

Confidence   Competence

When you take the time to educate yourself and become competent in your profession and company, you will feel increased confidence in your own ability to lead. Your employees will also see that despite your experience and competence, you still allow them to be the experts at their job while providing them with the tools and space to do so. This is leading with humility. With that competence, combined with humility, suddenly your employees will become confident in you as a leader and will trust your judgment.

In continuing with our comparison to vehicles, you are allowing your employees to drive the car that best suits their needs and responsibilities. You may not be the expert in how a sedan works, but you are competent enough to know how to diagnose and perform proper maintenance on the car to keep it running at peak performance.

Let's add another component to our example. As a leader, you provide the proper vehicle, but you also set boundaries, limits, and rules on how your employee should drive. Just like everyone on the road has to follow traffic signals, signs, speed limits, and other laws, your employees must drive within your policies and limits. If you set a goal for them to drive a 500 mile race to the next deadline, you don't need them to drive 600 miles so they can claim they went the furthest. You need everyone on the same page and racing the same track.

We can liken this to different leadership or driving modes. Many cars come with different modes built in. With modern technology, a small sedan can have a standard mode, an economy mode, and a sport mode. Each one of these modes changes the way the engine operates to react to different driving situations. As a leader, you set these modes with your employees.

Race Mode, Sport mode—This mode is designed for the short-term bursts of energy needed to meet a deadline, complete a task, or push out an order. It may require asking employees to put in extra time, stay late, and really focus. This mode is highly effective at getting things done quickly, but as a result can cause burnout. A car can overheat and will burn more fuel when in this mode. As a leader, you must recognize that race mode is not sustainable. It can be motivating and energizing in short-term bursts, but shouldn't be a long-term strategy. If you find yourself operating in this mode too often, you need to reevaluate your resources and your tasks. You may need to go up the leadership chain to fight for more employees or more reasonable demands. As race mode should be seldom used, you need to remember to show appreciation and reward your employees when you do require it. When the burst of energy is done, your employees may need a day off or some sort of way to decompress from the stress.

Race Mode Rule: If you are going to ask your employees to enter race mode, you have to be right there with them. If you go home after asking them to work late, they will grow to resent you and lose confidence in your ability to lead.

A racecar is engineered to handle the intense demands of the race track. The cooling system, brakes, engine, safety measures, and many more items are modified to handle its demands. Even with the modifications, racecars don't last long before they need a complete overhaul. How are you training your employees to handle race mode situations? How are you modifying their job requirements to help them be successful during race time? Are you communicating your expectations? Finally, are you carefully watching the instrument panel so that you can fix problems before they become catastrophic failures? A blown tire is much worse at 200 miles an hour than it is at 20.

Economy Mode - Economy mode is where you want to be most of the time. Your goal should be to create an environment where each employee is working at maximum efficiency. You do this by following the precepts taught in this book. You have allowed every employee to drive the vehicle that fits their needs and style so that they will be productive and engaged. You have created an environment where they can thrive on a daily basis. You have carefully placed each employee in the right role, with the right responsibilities, and with clear expectations. You have allowed everyone to be an expert in their field. You have created trusted avenues of communication, repair, and maintenance.

As a car drives down the road, each component has been programmed to do its specific job to help the vehicle arrive safely at its destination. The driver drives with confidence, constantly monitoring the dashboard indicators and the feel of the road. The leader does not have to think about how many times the engine needs to fire per minute or if the engine is getting its proper air-to-fuel mixture, they just need to provide the roadmap, designate the route, and monitor all of the other vehicles as they move toward the final destination.

Maintenance Mode - Every vehicle requires maintenance. If you keep up with preventative maintenance, you can avoid many major problems, but not all. Remember the vehicle with over 500,000 miles referenced earlier? During the life of that car, the engine was rebuilt at least once and the transmission was replaced. You can't just change the oil and expect a car to run for a half a million miles. Cars, and people, don't work that way.

As problems arise, your car sends signals telling you that it needs repairs or maintenance. Some maintenance can be foreseen, but not all. As a leader, you can consider yourself the fleet manager. As you oversee your fleet of vehicles, you should be constantly ensuring maintenance is being done and problems are fixed right away. You can't put off repairs because you don't have time or it is too inconvenient.

Marcus

> My father-in-law rebuilt the engine of that 500,000 mile vehicle before the engine seized up and died. He recognized signs in the way the car was driving and decided to move forward with the rebuild before something catastrophic happened.

That's an example of a large fix, but the same thing applies to small problems. Train your team to recognize and communicate problems early so they can be fixed right away.

You will face the inevitable problem whether an employee is not producing or worse, is killing morale through bad behavior or a bad attitude. Most situations have a solution. Often, the problem can be fixed with the right people, patience, and experience. But don't forget, getting rid of the problem is sometimes the best solution. Insurance companies frequently "total" a car that would cost more to repair than it's worth. Despite your desire to help everyone succeed, sometimes the lesson an employee needs is simple: failure happens.

Eric

> When my mechanics start to get angry or frustrated at a car that they are working on, I tell them to step away and cool off. Otherwise, the car will always win. The car does not care if a mechanic is getting frustrated that a part doesn't fit quite right or a bolt is stuck. When an employee is causing frustration, take a step back. Look at the situation from another angle. Ask another colleague for advice. Unlike a car, the employee will show emotion and must be treated with professionalism and care. But ultimately, both of you want the car back up and running.

> I was an Emergency Medical Technician (EMT) for 14 years and had to be prepared for anything. Often, I would get good information in advance, but otherwise I had to react to whatever I found at the scene as it happened. I knew I had to be calm as I assessed the situation and began treating the injured. My mood affected the patients as well as the rest of my crew. I can cite many situations when a crew member escalated the situation through their attitude and behavior, causing the patient to become combative and uncooperative. That didn't help anyone.

The most important thing to remember, especially in Maintenance Mode, is to act with humility. Look at the totality of the situation and change gears so that your employee can get back up to speed. Give them the time and resources they need to get back to working efficiently. Be open to suggestions and feedback as you search for ways to help fix the situation and avoid it in the future. Be willing to make changes and admit that maybe your Economy Mode procedures need adjusting for the long haul ahead.

Maybe you thought you were in Economy Mode, but your employees felt like they were in Race Mode.

If you have shown that you are responsive to diagnostic indicators, your employees will come to you with problems before they become catastrophes, and hopefully you can fix things and get back on the road before you need to take the car into the shop for a week. When employees start to feel burned out, or like their gas tank is sitting on empty, look from their perspective. They may shift between Race Mode and Economy Mode at a different RPM than you do. You may not have communicated your expectations effectively.

As a leader, you must train yourself to step back, look at the entire situation from every angle, and then come up with the best solution without using intimidation, threats, or anger.

Chapter 11

Driving to Success

E ven if you don't drive, chances are you find yourself in some sort of vehicle on a regular basis—be it a ride share, taxi, or commuter van. From here on out, everytime you climb into a vehicle, think about what kind of leader you are at work. Every time the seat belt light flashes or the low fuel light comes on, think about how you respond to problems at work. Have you created an environment where your employees are sending those signals to you as soon as they sense a problem? Or are you the guy who tore out the fuse to the dashboard so you wouldn't have to be bothered by any of those pesky lights?

The biggest problem with books or programs designed to help you become a better leader is that the people who desperately need to learn the principles being taught believe they are already doing everything right. They don't need the help. Don't let that become you. No matter how well you treat your fleet of vehicles, you will have cars that break down on you.

You probably have already created a mission statement, a vision statement, and even annual goals for your business. If that happened above your head, they have been passed down to you as expectations. Even if you aren't the CEO and don't get to decide the direction of the entire fleet, you do have the ability to create goals for your own team—and especially for your own vehicle. You get to set your destination and how you are going to get there, especially if your boss has given you the car that fits your role and needs.

When we break it down to the bare bones, a driver has to do three things before driving off: turn the key, shift into gear, hit the gas. Thousands of signals and explosions are happening because of those actions, but those are the things a driver has to do to go anywhere.

Turn the key = TRUST

We've already talked about expectations regarding our vehicles. We trust that our cars are going to work, and they trust we will operate and maintain them properly. We trust the engine will fire up when we turn the key.

Trust goes both ways. All of us were hired to a job based on our specific skill set, education, and experience. Whether you were recruited or you responded to a job announcement, you were deemed the best person for the job by the people who interviewed you and reviewed your qualifications.

Your company trusts you to do that job and bring that expertise to the table. They trust you will give it your all and that you will fill that hole that they identified when they first created your position.

On the other hand, you trust that the job advertisement was accurate and you will be doing the job you signed up to do. You trust that your company will give you the tools and resources to do the job they expected you to do.

You wouldn't try to tow a boat with a sports car, and you definitely wouldn't take your truck to a drag race.

Leaders, listen up. Use your employees wisely. Don't erode their trust by putting them in the wrong position.

Trust also dictates that we, that all of us, act like a sensor in a car. Just as a sensor is tasked with monitoring a specific function in a car and then sending that information back to the computer, you are responsible for letting your leaders know when something is broken or needs to be fixed. They trust you to let them know.

Unfortunately, that trust doesn't always translate to communication, which leads us to our next point.

Shift Into Gear = COMMUNICATION

Everyone talks about communication, but few people do it well. Let's turn to our vehicle for advice on how to communicate. When you shift gears, you are telling the vehicle you are ready to go, and in which direction. As you are driving down the road, you and your car are constantly communicating with each other, even when you are speeding down the freeway. You constantly make minor adjustments with the steering wheel—to avoid bumps, obstacles, and just to keep you straight between the lane lines. Roads are not built perfectly flat, so if you let go of the steering wheel for any length of time, eventually you will end up in the wrong lane or off the road completely. These adjustments are so small and constant you don't even realize you are making them.

You also tell the car when it's too hot or too cold by adjusting the air. You adjust the stereo. You adjust the mirrors.

All the while, your car is communicating with you as well. Obviously, the dashboard or screen will show errors and warnings, just like we talked about, but your car is saying much more than that. The engine makes a certain sound when it is running at peak efficiency. The belt will screech and whine to tell you it needs to be tightened or replaced. Your tires will tell you through sound and vibration if they need to be changed.

The biggest barrier to communication in the workplace isn't the lack of words. We talk. We text. We email. We write memos. We use body language. We already do all of that. The single biggest problem we face in effective communication is a lack of humility.

Humility is a communication skill.

Remember the owner of the vintage truck who was convinced he needed his motor mounts replaced? We often think we know best, or worse, that our coworker is ignorant, and therefore we fail to listen. When you remove humility from a conversation, you remove the ability to understand and empathize with the other person's point of view.

This seems to be a particular problem with new or insecure leaders. They believe they have something to prove and by virtue of their job have been endowed from on high with all knowledge pertaining to every job in the company. Ridiculous. Remember, leaders, every employee was hired because they are an expert in their field. If you were the expert, you would have their job, not yours. Approach every conversation with humility and just watch the barriers fall.

You will be amazed at how many employees suddenly have valuable input to share.

Press the Gas = ACTION

In the immortal words of Charlie Daniels, what this world needs is "a little less talk and a lot more action." As your communication skills improve through humility and more people feel safe coming to speak with you, recognize that what they are really doing is investing in their job, which in turn is an investment in the company.

Anyone who cares enough to provide feedback to either improve the workplace or your product is investing in the company. They want to believe in the job they are doing. People want to feel proud of the work they do.

It doesn't matter what job you have; you can feel pride in your work because you are performing a vital task for someone.

Marcus

> I lived in Sicily for three years. Neighborhoods there could go weeks without trash pickup because of corruption and organized crime. I am now eternally grateful for the men and women who pick up my trash every week. I'm grateful for the teenager who hands me my bag of food with a smile and genuinely tells me to have a good day.

People who care about their job, who are invested in their company, will produce better and higher results. So why are we as leaders so adept at creating miserable employees instead of happy ones?

The key is leading by action. When you turn your steering wheel to tell the car to turn right, it does not respond with a message stating, "Thank you for your input. I will take it under advisement and bring it up at the next meeting." No! It turns the wheel.

On the other hand, when the check engine light comes on, you don't run a focus group to decide whether or not to take the car into the shop. You believe what your car is telling you and take action.

Is all this to say that you have to implement every suggestion immediately? Of course not. Some suggestions might be good, but only beneficial to a few employees instead of the whole team. Other suggestions may not align with your goals. That's fine. If that's the case, communicate. Explain why.

Sometimes a suggestion is big enough that you do have to take it to your boss or the board. Communicate that and then do it and follow up.

> "Hey, Susan, remember your suggestion from last week? Well, we had a supervisor's meeting this morning and I had it put on the agenda. We had a great discussion about it and they would like you to put together some additional data projections..."

Maybe it will never be implemented, but Susan knows you took action and did everything you could. She trusts you. You listened, communicated, and took action.

The goal is to lead a successful business by building the best widget or providing the best service. You do this by hiring and retaining the best people, which in turn requires your employees to feel happy, fulfilled, engaged, and needed.

Happiness

Engagement   Retention

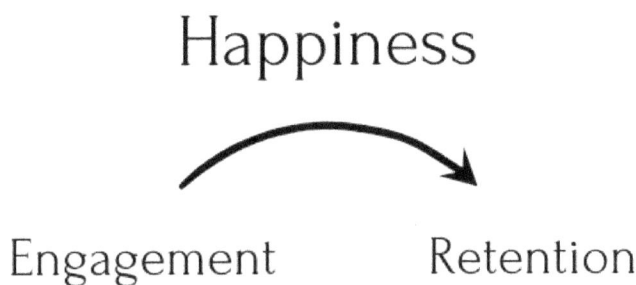

Find the best person for the role you need filled and then give that person the car they will love to drive. Provide clear and transparent expectations along with all of the tools they need to accomplish their assignment, and then get out of the road.

Be ready with air, oil, washer fluid, or whatever else they need to keep driving ahead so that you can get things fixed and back on the road as quickly as possible. Know when to jump into race mode and when to slow down into maintenance mode.

You are managing a fleet of very different, individual cars driven by unique and talented individuals. Keep the cars shined and in tip-top shape and you will be surprised at how far and fast they will go.

There is no reason for employees to feel so depressed and unengaged at work. We spend our entire childhood dreaming of what we want to be when we grow up. Why does it have to be a disappointment? Here's the truth: it doesn't. We can feel excited about going to work again. We can feel fulfilled at work again. We can be happy in our jobs. With the right perspective, we can sit down behind the wheel, turn the key, and listen to the engine roar.